Kindle Fire HDX Tips, Tricks and Traps

Learn How to Use Your Kindle Fire HDX Effortlessly!

Disclaimer

© Michael K Edwards

Are you looking for a tablet that is best for both work and play? A tablet that is not only good for reading books or work related documents but is also perfect for playing games and watching videos or movies? A tablet that is both highly functional plus aesthetically appealing? If yes, then Kindle Fire HDX is just the tablet that you are looking for.

But how can you make the most out of a gadget if you know nothing about it or do not have enough time to explore it? This eBook is your answer to that because we have laid it out for you. In this book you will find all that you need to know about your Kindle Fire HDX, all the tips, tricks, traps, and what not. You name it, we have it. This book includes:

1. Basic information that you need to get started.
2. Tips, tricks and traps regarding the new and improved features of Kindle Fire HDX.
3. Ways to increase the usability and functionality of your tablet.

So continue reading this book to learn all about your Kindle Fire HDX.

Contents

Introduction

Kindle Fire HDX is an amazing new tablet launched by Amazon and it comes packed with features that has placed it in the league of the market leaders. Its quad core processor, Dolby audio, HDX display and improved battery life will enhance just about any experience for you. Whether you want to read your favorite book, watch your favorite movie, play your favorite game, or listen to your favorite song Kindle Fire HDX is a perfect gadget for all.

Kindle Fire HDX is the perfect gadget for the whole family, whether you want to enhance your child's learning experience or enjoy a movie with a loved one, this is the gadget to have. But using a gadget that is new to you can be very unnerving because simple things such as customizing the settings, downloading or deleting content can be difficult if you are not familiar with the functions of the tablet. Therefore, in this book we will spell out for you each and every detail that will help you use your Kindle Fire HDX to the fullest and make the most of all its features.

Read along to get acquainted with your Kindle Fire HDX and enter the world of innovation.

Chapter 1 – Getting To Know Your Kindle

Kindle Fire HDX is the latest tablet introduced by Amazon.com and in this section we will be discussing a brief history of Kindle and a take a look inside its box.

What Are Tablet Computers?

Tablet computers, commonly known as tablets, are mobile computers that contain battery, circuitry, and display all in one unit. Tablets have touch screens, accelerometer, microphone, camera and sensors. You can use them with a stylus or fingers which eliminates the need of keyboards and mouse. Tablets also include physical buttons to control the basic functions such as volume control and power button. They have a virtual pop-up keyboard which is used for typing. Tablets are larger than PDA (personal digital assistants) and smart phones with 7 inch or larger displays when measured diagonally.

Tablet computers have made it extremely easy for people to stay connected on the go since you can take them anywhere with you. They come with in-built storage that allows you to access your data wherever and whenever you want. The ease of use and functionality of tablets have made them very popular among people and that is the reason why many brands out there are trying to capture the market with new and improved tablet computers.

Kindle Fire HDX is one such tablet computer, by Amazon.com, which comes packed with amazing and enhanced features which is why it is now in the lead with the market leaders.

A Brief History of Kindle Fire HD

Reading kindles a fire in the minds and hearts of passionate readers and this is why Michael Cronan and his partner Karin Hibma thought that this was the perfect name for a tablet that is a perfect reading tool.

1st Generation

Kindle

Screenshot courtesy: Amazon.com

The first Kindle was introduced in 2007 and it was sold out in less than six hours of its introduction. This device had a 4-level grayscale display with an audio jack that also allowed the users to access audio files on their Kindle. The device had an internal memory of 250 MB which could store 200 non-illustrated books approximately and came with an SD card slot to expand its memory.

2nd Generation

Kindle 2

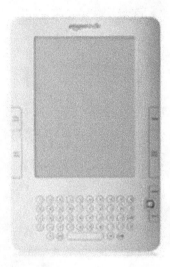

Screenshot courtesy: Amazon.com

Amazon introduced Kindle 2 in 2009 and it came with the options new features such as reading the text aloud, and text-to-speech. It was slightly slimmer than the previous Kindle and had an internal memory of 2 GB out of which 1.4 GB was accessible to the user and there was no room for an SD card slot. According to Amazon's estimation it had the capacity to store 1500 non-illustrated titles.

Kindle DX

Screenshot courtesy: Amazon.com

This version of Kindle was also announced by Amazon in 2009 and is by far the thinnest version of Kindle. It comes with a large screen and supports simple files of PDF format. It has an accelerometer that allows the reader to switch between landscape and portrait orientation for reading.

Kindle DX Graphite

Screenshot courtesy: Amazon.com

This was announced in 2010 and it comes with an E Ink Pearl technology which gives it 50% better ratio of contrast. This version is a combination of 2nd generation software and 3rd generation hardware. It support MP3 playback and text-to-speech features.

3rd Generation

Kindle Keyboard

Screenshot courtesy: Amazon.com

This was announced in 2010 and has a 6 inch screen with 600x800 screen resolution. It is available in two versions; one that can connect to the internet only through Wi-Fi, and the other that has both Wi-Fi and 3G connectivity which allowed its user to download content on-the-go.

4th Generation

Kindle

Screenshot courtesy: Amazon.com

This tablet was announced by Amazon in 2011 and has an e-ink 6 inch display with web browsing features. It comes with one month battery life, 2GB memory, touch keyboard, cursor pad, and nine hard keys.

Kindle Touch

Screenshot courtesy: Amazon.com

Kindle touch was also announced in 2011 and was available in two version; once with a Wi-Fi, and the other with 3G connectivity along with Wi-Fi. It has a battery life of two month and a touch screen with E-ink technology.

5th Generation

Kindle

This was the latest version of Kindle Paperwhite and Kindle and was introduced by Amazon in 2012. It was 15% faster with 167 PPI display and it is by far the lightest Kindle at 170 grams (5.98 oz).

Kindle Paperwhite (1st Generation)

Screenshot courtesy: Amazon.com

This was released in 2010 and has a 212 ppi, 6 inch display. It has a built-in storage of 2 GB and is available in two versions: one with Wi-Fi only, and the other with 3G connectivity plus Wi-Fi.

6th Generation

Kindle Paperwhite (2nd Generation)

This is referred to as the new Paperwhite and was introduced in 2013. It comes with 25% faster processor, LED light and E-ink display technology.

Which Generation Of Kindle Do You Own?

Screenshot courtesy: Amazon.com

Kindle Fire HDX belongs to the third generation of Kindle Fire line introduced by Amazon. This came into the market on 25th September, 2013 and took the market by storm with it new and improved features. This tablet is also available in two versions: one with that connects only through Wi-Fi while the other that comes with 3G connectivity along with Wi-Fi options. There are two models of Kindle fire HDX; one is 8.9 inch and the other is 7 inches.

Inside the Box

Kindle Fire HDX comes in stylish packaging of matt black and thin box. Amazon defines its packaging as hassle free as it a single piece of cardboard that has been folded in the shape of a box to hold the new Kindle Fire HDX. You can open the box easily by pulling a tab. The box itself is covered in a plastic wrap. All you need to do to reveal your new Kindle Fire HDX is to remove the plastic cover and pull the tab to open the box.

Inside the packaging you will find you Kindle placed center and front. Above the tablet is a small box with flaps that contains microUSB cable and the charger. The initial instructions to start your Kindle can be found beneath the tablet. There are no thick guides, or warranty information to distract you from your new tablet. You can just switch on your device and start exploring. Amazon has kept the packaging nice and simple this time.

Getting Started On Your Kindle HDX

Now that you have taken out your tablet from the box, it is time that you switch it on. Once you start the tablet it will connect to your Amazon account automatically. Following are the easy steps that you can follow to start your Kindle Fire HDX:

1. Switch on the device by pressing the power button.
2. To unlock swipe the lock icon from side to center of the screen.
3. Select the language that you want you want your Kindle Fire HDX to operate in and continue.
4. Select your Wi-Fi network from the options and enter your password to get connected. Tap the option of "Connect" to get started.
5. Now you can instantly log in to your social network sites such as Facebook or Twitter.
6. Type in your password and username to stay connected to your social media account.
7. In case you do not have these accounts or do not want to connect then tap the "Next" button to move on to the next part.
8. You should now be on your main screen. Tap the option of "Get Started" to learn some basic functions such as getting back to the "Carousel" switching between applications etc.

This are just the basic steps that you need to follow in order to get comfortable with the device and start exploring.

Where Is Your Data Being Stored?

Kindle Fire HDX comes in 16/32/64 GB in-built storage which is not expandable. But this is not all because Kindle Fire HDX gives you an amazing option of storing your Data in Cloud drive where you can store anything digital and access it from anywhere you want. It is not only convenient to have your data stored in cloud drive from where you can access it anytime and anywhere but it is also a safe because all your important documents and memories are protected in cloud drive.

Relive the memories by saving your videos and photos in cloud drive and keep them close to your heart. You can easily access all your data by using Kindle Fire documents application and the best part is that all the videos and pictures that you take from your Kindle Fire HDX are directly stored in the cloud Drive.

Now that you know where your data is being stored, it is time to look at the basic layouts and designs of 1st and 2nd generation Kindle HD.

Layout and Controls of Kindle Fire HD – First Generation

Powering up!

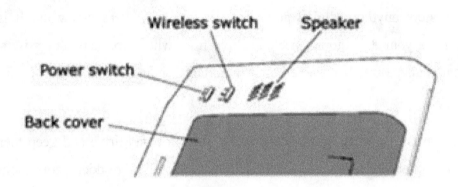

Screenshot courtesy: Amazon.com

Push the power switch on the back of your 1st generation Kindle tablet in the on position. You might have to charge the battery if you are using it right out of the box.

Select Wheel

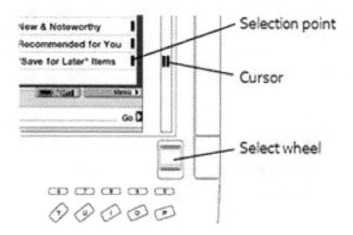

Screenshot courtesy: Amazon.com

The select wheel in 1st generation Kindle tablet is used to scroll the cursor up and down the page. To select a specific point on the page all you need to do is to move the cursor to that point and push the select wheel inwards single time.

Reading Layout

The experience of reading a book on 1st generation tablets of Kindle Fire is very much like reading from a real book. The layout includes the table of contents, the chapters, prologue and so onward. Every page contains a header displaying the name of the book, the author's name or the date of issue.

At the bottom of the page you will find the location numbers, progress indicator, wireless indicator, and global battery. Locations are page numbers and they might be different depending on the size of the text that you have chosen for reading.

Layout and Controls of Kindle Fire HD – Second Generation

Powering up!

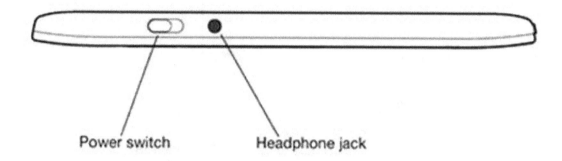

Power switch   Headphone jack

Screenshot courtesy: Amazon.com

The power switch shown in the image is used for multiple purposes such as switching on or waking up your Kindle. To turn on your table you need to slide and release the power button. To put your Kindle to sleep you need to slide and release the power button. To switch off your tablet you need to slide and hold the button for about 4 seconds and release when the screen goes blank. The power button on your Kindle can also reset your device. Disconnect the tablet from the power source and then hold the power button for about 15 seconds to reset.

Getting Around Your Kindle

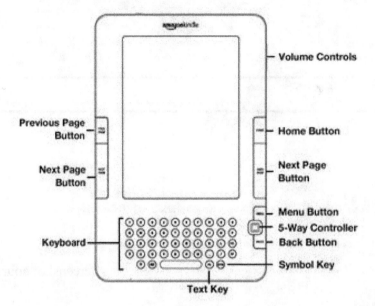

Screenshot courtesy: Amazon.com

This is a simple diagram that will give you the basic information about how you can move around your Kindle.

Now that you have been formerly introduced to the Kindle Fire HDX it is time that we dive into its depths. Read along to know more about the third generation Kindle Fire HDX.

Chapter 2 – User Interface

Now that you know all about getting started with your new Kindle Fire HDX, we will now discuss some of its basic setting, functions, and features.

Setting Up Home Screen, Carousel, Navigation Bar, and Favorites

Screenshot Courtesy: Amazon.com

Once you are done with the initial setup like explained above, you now need to access the home screen. To do that you need to tap the Home button. On home screen you will see a carousel containing the recent applications that you accessed and thumbnails of the books you are reading. To browse through the content of the carousel you need to swipe or flip through it and you simply need to tap on an item to access it. You cannot change the order of the items, with which they appear on the carousel because the recently accessed item will always appear fist on it.

Navigation Bar

There are many different libraries accessible on the Kindle fire store and the navigation bar gives you a quick access to each one of them. You simple need to tap the navigation bar to access a content library. Once you select a category the carousel will show content included in that library only. To browse through the navigation bar you simply need to swipe of across the menu.

Screenshot courtesy: Amazon.com

Quick links are also available at the bottom of the page. It shows content related to the app showing at the middle of the carousel. For example, if carousel shows a movie at the center then the quick links will include the links to the movies that the other buyers have bought from Amazon. Quick links may also include the list of the tasks included in the application that is being displayed on the carousel.

How to Add Item in the Favorites List?

There is a star icon present in the lower right corner on your screen; the list of your favorite item will appear when you tap this icon. Adding item to your favorites will allow you to access most used items easily. Following are the simple steps of adding item on your favorite list:

1. Press and hold the icon of the application or book that you want to add in your favorites list.
2. Tap "add to favorites" from the menu.
3. Tap the star (favorite icon) on the lower right corner.

The list of your favorite icons will appear below the carousel.

Display

Following are some of the basic display setting that you need to be familiar with in order to set up your display:

Screen Orientation

Kindle Fire HDX comes with an accelerometer which means that it can sense the direction in which you are holding the device and automatically adjust the screen. Sometimes you want to stop this from happening, for example when you are reading a book in portrait mode. However, there are orientation will change automatically to landscape mode when you are watching video so it is not always your choice. You can prevent the orientation from changing by following the simple given steps:

1. Access the settings drawer by swiping down the status bar when your screen is on your desired orientation.
2. Tap the "unlocked" icon to lock the orientation and to prevent it from changing. The icon will change to "lock" after you tap it.

Brightness

The screen of the Kindle Fire HDX uses the battery more than any other thing on the tablet and the brighter the display the more battery it will consume. You can preserve your battery life for longer by changing the display settings in the following way:

1. Access the settings drawer by swiping down the status bar.
2. Tap on "brightness" icon.
3. Swipe the brightness control to left or right to adjust the desired level of brightness.

Customizing and Selecting Favorites

Rearranging Your Favorite Icons

You can easily rearrange icons in your favorite list according to your preference because they appear in the order that you add them. Following are the steps in which you can rearrange the icons easily:

1. Press and hold the icon that you want to move around. Do not lift your finger from the icon even if you see a menu pop up.
2. Drag the icon to the location where you want to place it.
3. Move your finger and release the icon.

Removing an Item from the Favorites

Removing an item from your favorites list is as simple as adding it.

1. Press and hold the icon that you want to remove from your favorite list.
2. Tap "remove from favorites" from the options.

Toggle with the Basic Settings

We will be discussing more settings as we go along but following are some of the basic settings that will help you get familiarize with your new Kindle Fire HDX.

Volume

There are buttons for adjusting the volume on the device. Pressing these buttons shows you the volume meter on the screen as well. However, you can adjust the volume directly from the screen as well.

1. Access the settings drawer by swiping down the status bar.
2. Tap the volume icon to access the volume controls.
3. Swipe the control to the left or right to decrease to increase the volume respectively.

Device Information

To look for information such as the version of operating system, used and remaining storage space, remaining percentage of the battery etc. you need to access the device screen in the following way:

1. Access the settings drawer by swiping down the status bar.
2. Tap the icon of "more".
3. Tap the icon of "device".
4. The device screen will appear on your screen and you can now just simply tap the icon that you want information about like the "battery" or "storage".

When you tap "storage" the storage screen will display. This screen will give you information about the space being occupied by different types of data such as music, audio books, or videos.

Wi-Fi

Sometimes you may want to turn off your Wi-Fi depending on where you are. It also consumes less battery so you can also turn it off when you don't want to stay connected to the internet. To turn off Wi-Fi you just need to do the following:

1. Access the settings drawer by swiping down the status bar.
2. Tap the icon of "wireless".
3. Tap "off" icon to turn the Wi-Fi off. Tap on" to turn it back on.

Tips for Typing and Text Entry

Kindle fire HDX has a touch to type keyboard and it is just like any other keyboard that you use in your smart phones or computers. Using the keyboard frequently to write documents or emails will get you more used to enter data using the touch keyboard.

Typing Text

Entering text via your Kindle Fire keyboard is pretty simple and get more convenient with some new features:

1. To enter text, tap on the space where you want to add text such as a document or an email.
2. Tap the letter on you're the keyboard that appears on the bottom of the screen to enter text.
3. As you type suggested words will appear. You can tap a suggested word to enter that word.

You can use some shortcuts like tapping the shift key twice to type in caps lock or tapping the space key twice to add a period at the end of a sentence.

Cursor

Alphabets are added where you have positioned your cursor. You can easily go back to a point in a sentence of you want to add or delete text. You can reposition your cursor in the following way:

1. Tap once in the area where you are entering text.
2. Tap on the position where you want your cursor indicator to move.

Editing and Selecting Text

This option helps you remove a block of text that you entered instead of deleting one character at a time.

1. Tap twice on the text that you have entered.
2. Drag the right indicator to the end of the passage of word that you want to change or delete.
3. Type to replace or press backspace to delete the selection.

Cut/Copy and Paste

In case you have to cut/copy or paste text someplace else. You can do that by following the given steps:

1. Tap twice on the text that you want to copy or cut.
2. Drag the right indicator to the end of the passage to select.
3. Press cut or copy option.
4. Press and hold the space where you want to paste the selection.
5. Press "paste".

Numbers and Punctuations

Using punctuations or numbers during an email or document is not uncommon. Here is how you can add symbols, numbers, or punctuations in your text.

1. There is a number key on the keypad. Tap that so that the keyboard displays punctuation marks, and numbers.
2. To display symbols, press the symbol button on the keyboard.
3. To enter a symbol, punctuation mark, or a number you just simply have to tap on it.
4. To return to the alphabets keyboard, tap the button with ABC written on it.

Diacriticals and Accent Marks

In case you are typing in foreign language such as French, you will need to add diacriticals and accent marks to certain characters. These letters are often vowels and n and c.

1. Press and hold the letter on which you want to add the accent.
2. Do not lift your finger and slide it across the character and release to enter.

These were some of the basic tools that you can make use of while type text on your Kindle Fire HDX.

Chapter 3 – Music, Movies, And Books

Now that you know how to get started with your Kindle Fire HDX, it is time that we look into some other details. With its amazing HDX display Kindle fire takes you a step ahead of HD. The video and audio experience of Kindle Fire is incomparable and it comes with a unique feature that allows perfect viewing experience both indoors and outdoors.

In this chapter we will be discussing in detail about how to play music and videos on your Kindle and how to get started on reading your favorite books on your tablet.

How to Play Music on Your Kindle

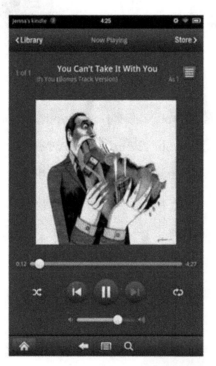

Screenshot Courtesy: Amazon.com

To listen to your favorite music on Kindle simple tap and hold the song, album, artist, or playlist and tap on "Now Playing" button. This will queue the song in the list of songs that you are currently listening to.

Once you reach the end of your "Now Playing" list, it will clear automatically. If you want to save a list of music for playback, you must create a playlist.

Finding Music

There is an icon of a magnifying glass at the end of your screen, tap that icon and type the name of the song, album, or artist that you want to search. The search result matching with the word that you have entered in the search field will appear on your screen.

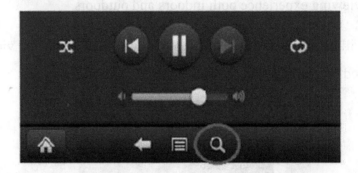

Screenshot Courtesy: Amazon.com

You can search for music that is on your device or in your Cloud storage. Cloud includes all the music that you have downloaded in your Cloud player whereas the device tab contains the songs that you have downloaded in your tablet. The downloaded music can be played without the internet access.

Playback Controls

When a song is playing on the tablet, you will be able to see an art view, or picture of the song. On this screen you will find the shuffle button, next, pause/play, previous etc. You will also find a repeat button on the lower left corner of the screen. You can tap this to repeat the song or the entire "Now Playing" list.

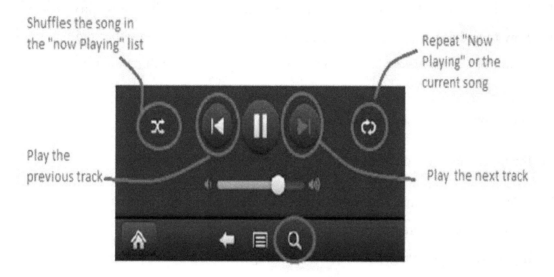

Screenshot Courtesy: Amazon.com

Managing and Creating Playlist

In order to create a playlist, you need to follow the given steps:

1. Tap **library** button.
2. Press the option of **Playlists**.
3. Select the option of "**Create New Playlist**".
4. Type in the name that you want to give to your playlist and then press **Save**.
5. Now to add songs in the playlist that you have created you can either tap the orange plus button or use the search bar to look up the songs or artists that you want to add in your playlist.
6. Once you are done selecting the songs, press **Done**.

Follow the given steps, if you want to edit the Playlist that you created:

1. Select the playlist that you want to edit and then press Edit. This will allow you to see all the songs that are present in this playlist.
2. If you want to rearrange the sequence of songs on the playlist, you can do this by pressing the song that you want to move and dragging and dropping it. You can even do this by tapping the **drag and drop** button present on the left side of every song.
3. Press the **minus** button present on the right side of every song in order to remove the song from your playlist.
4. In order to delete the complete playlist, you need to tap and hold the playlist that you want to delete and then tap "**Delete Playlist**" option.

This option will only delete the playlist, but not the songs that were in the playlist. In order to delete a song or an album from your tablet you need to tap that song and hold, then select the option of delete.

Playing Videos on Kindle

Playing videos is very simple on your Kindle Fire HDX. If you have already downloaded the video on your tablet that on you need to do is press Videos button, then go to library, search for the video or movie that you want to play and tap on it to play. In case you have played this particular video before you will have to tap the resume button. Start over if you want to watch it from the start.

Screenshot Courtesy: Amazon.com

In case you are streaming video stored in your Cloud storage then you need to follow the given steps:

1. Tap **Videos** on the home screen of your Kindle Fire HDX.
2. You will find a **library** button on your screen in the top right side.
3. Press the tab of Cloud. This will display the videos that you have purchased or rented and whose rental date has not been expired yet.
4. Press on any item that you want to play.

    In case you want to watch a TV show you will see the list of episodes in that season. Tap on an episode to open it or press the **Buy** button to purchase the complete season.

Screenshot Courtesy: Amazon.com

In case you want to watch a movie, tap on it to see the description of the movie and to get the option or downloading it or watching it.

5. Press the **Watch Now** button. Now you will be able to see the playback control.

6. In case you have already watched some part of the movie, press the **Resume** button.

   If you want to watch the movies from the beginning then tap the **Play from Beginning** key.

   You will be able to watch the video on the whole screen while you can see the title of the video at the base of the screen.

Accessing Video Controls

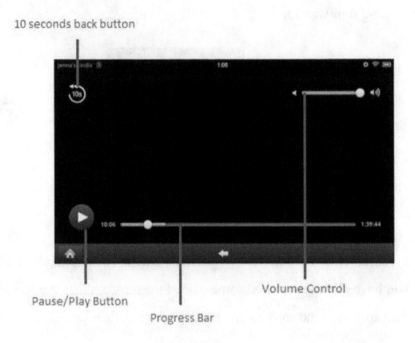

Screenshot Courtesy: Amazon.com

You can access these controls by tapping on the screen while the video is playing.

1. Slide your finger right or left over the volume control bar in order to decrease or increase the volume.

2. Press the Pause/Play button to resume or play a video.

3. The "10 seconds back" button on the top of the screen will rewind the video by 10 seconds.

4. To move forward or backward in the video you need to slide your finger left or right on the scroll bar respectively.

Deleting Videos

If you want to free some storage space on your tablet you can delete some videos. To do so you need to follow the given steps:

1. Tap **Video** on home screen.
2. Tap **Library.**
3. Then look for the detail page of the video.
4. Tap the option of Delete in the download box.

Following these steps will only delete the video from your tablet. It will not be deleted from your cloud storage from where you can download it again to watch.

Get Books from Your Kindle from Your Local Library

Now that you have learned about how to play music and videos, it is time that we discuss about how to read your favorite books on Kindle.

You can now read your favorite books with Kindle Fire HDX without even setting foot in your local library. More than 11,000 libraries across United States and 27,000 public schools and libraries worldwide, allow you to borrow books from your Public Library on your Kindle. All you need to do is to look at the website of the library, find the eBook that you are looking for and ask them to send the eBook directly to your reading application or Kindle.

Just like a normal library book, the books that you download from the Kindle Library are also available to your for a limited period of time. You can get these eBooks via Overdrive which is a digital service.

You can read Kindle books on all application of Kindle that are free, or on your web browser that has a Cloud Reader, or any generation of Kindle tablets. All you need to do it follow the given steps.

1. Confirm whether the branch of your local library carries eBooks for Kindle and is eligible or not. To find it visit the website of your local library or look on Overdrive.
2. Get a PIN and a library card from your Public Local Library.

Returning a Book

In order to return a book before the borrowing period expires you need to visit "Manage Your Kindle". Different library have different policies about the returning date and it varies from library to library. You need to check with your Public Library to find out their policies. You will get a courtesy e-mail three day before the expiry date of your borrowing period and then another mail when the period ends. To return a book you need to follow the given steps;

1. Go to **Manage Your Kindle.**
2. Next to the book that you have borrowed, tap the option of **Actions** and then press the option of **Return This Book.**

After the returning the book you will not be able to access it from your Kindle. However, you can access your highlights and save notes from **Manage Your Kindle**. In future if you buy the book again from Amazon, or borrow it from the library, your highlights and notes will appear on it.

All about KOLL – Kindle Owner's Lending Library

Kindle Owner's Lending Library has been introduced by Amazon and it allows the Kindle owners with Amazon prime to choose from over 500,000 books that they can borrow. Not only are these books free but they also have no due date.

How It Works?

This facility can only be availed by Kindle owners regardless of the generation of Kindle that they own. The next thing you need is a prime membership that allows you to get the benefit of free shipping in Two Days, plus access to more than 41,000 TV shows and movies. Having these to pre-requisites will allow you to enjoy over 350,000 titles of books that you can read on your Kindle for absolutely no cost at all.

Steps to Borrow

The following images will give you a step to step guideline about how to borrow books for free on your Kindle Fire:

Screenshot Courtesy: Amazon.com

You will find the Kindle Owner's Lending Library in the bookstore of Kindle Fire.

Screenshot Courtesy: Amazon.com

You can identify a book from Kindle Owner's Lending Library with the help of the Prime badge.

Screenshot Courtesy: Amazon.com

Select the option of **"Borrow for Free"** and start reading your favorite book. You can borrow a book at a time.

Search Free Books on Kindle Store

There are thousands of classics on kindle that you can read for free on our computer, Kindle, or other devices. Amazon provide a lot of old titles that are out-of-copyright and belonging to pre-1923 period which now consists of almost 2 million titles. Following are the instructions that you need to follow in order to find these classics and download them on your devices to read.

Kindle Store

There are thousands of popular classics on Kindle that you can choose from and which will be delivered to your device in less than 60 seconds through Whispernet. To find a book on Kindle store you need to:

1. Browse through the Kindle Most Popular Classics.
2. Find the title that you are searching for just like any other normal eBook on Kindle.

Internet Archive

This site contains more than 2.5 million free titles that you can download on your Kindle. It is a non-profit site dedicated to allowing people access to historical collections that is available in the digital format. To download these tiles you need to:

1. Visit the site archive.org.
2. Search for the title that you are looking for or narrow down your research by looking in one of the sub-collections.
3. While you are viewing the title that you need to download, you will see a button labeled "Kindle" on the left side of the title. Tap that to download file on your tablet.
4. If you have downloaded the title on your computer but want to read it on your Kindle all you need to do is connect your Kindle to your computer via USB cable and drag and drop the title in documents folder.
5. Open the book on your Kindle and experience the ultimate joy of reading on your Kindle.

There are other sites too such as gutenberg.org, manybooks.net, and openlibrary.org where you can find free title to read and enjoy on your Kindle tablet.

Chapter 4 – Silk Browser

In this section you will learn all about navigation and surfing the net with Silk Browser.

Screenshot Courtesy: Amazon.com

Surf with Silk

When you will open your Silk browser for the first time you find a collection of bookmarks that are most commonly used. You can simply tap on any of these sites to open them.

Screenshot Courtesy: Amazon.com

As you start using Silk browser more frequently you will see that the sites that you visit the most will start showing on your screen. You can clear these in the browsing history.

Screenshot Courtesy: Amazon.com

On silk browser you can browse a specific website or search a web by entering your search query in the search bar on top of the screen. Tap on the search bar and you will see the onscreen keyboard pop-up on your screen. Type in your term and tap the go button to initiate the search.

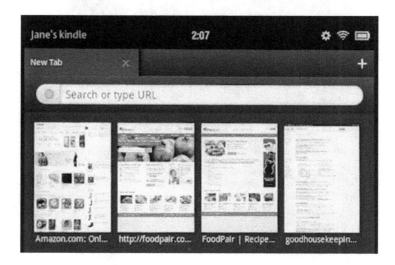

Screenshot Courtesy: Amazon.com

Screenshot Courtesy: Amazon.com

You can rotate your Kindle Fir to see a web browser in portrait or landscape mode. On the bottom right corner of the screen there is a full screen icon that you can tap to see the web pages in full screen mode. There will be an arrow at the end of the screen that you can tap to go back to the normal mode.

You can zoom in and out within the web page by pinching with your thumb and finger and in order to open item on the webpage you simply need to tap it once.

Screenshot Courtesy: Amazon.com

Create Bookmarks

It is really simple to create bookmarks on Silk browser. You need to follow the given steps in order to book mark a website:

1. There is a menu icon on the bottom of the screen that you need to tap in order to access the menu.

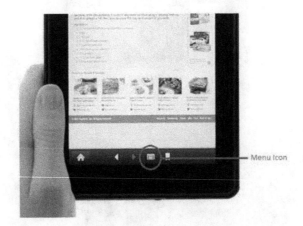

Screenshot Courtesy: Amazon.com

2. Press "Add Bookmark" option in the menu.

Screenshot Courtesy: Amazon.com

3. A dialogue box will appear in which you can type the default name of the site or any name that you want to give to the bookmark and press Ok.

Screenshot Courtesy: Amazon.com

To manage and view the bookmarks that you have created, press the icon of Bookmark that is present at the bottom of the screen. This will allow you to see a new screen containing all sites that you have bookmarked. Press and hold on any of the site to access more options.

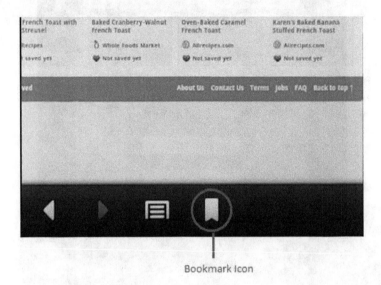

Bookmark Icon

Screenshot Courtesy: Amazon.com

Screenshot Courtesy: Amazon.com

There are icons on the top right of the screen through which you can change the view mood of the bookmarks to list of grid view.

Customize Setting

Customizing the setting of your silk browser is fairly easy. You can access the setting options by both tapping the Navigation Panel and then choosing the option of settings or by swiping the left edge of the page.

Screenshot Courtesy: Amazon.com

Following is a table containing information about all the basic and advanced setting of Silk browser in Kindle fire HDX.

Settings	Description
Search Engine	You can change the default search engine on your silk browser and select Yahoo!, Google, or Bing , according to your preference.
Block Pop-up Windows	• If you want the browser to notify you when it detects a pop-up window, tap **Ask.** •If you wan to allow pop-up windows on your silk browser, tap **Never.** •To permanently block pop-up windows on your silk browser, tap **Always.**
Accelerate Page Loading	This option will allow your Silk browser to make use of Amazon Cloud to load the web pages faster.
Option Encryption	Individual web requests are routed dynamically on the Silk Browser either through Amazon cloud or directly from the Kindle Fire. Tap on this option if you want the requests routed only through the servers of Amazon.
Enable Instant Page Loads	This option allows the Silk Browser upload the next page that you might visit faster than the usual page load. After choosing the cloud-accelerated link option you will see a lightning bolt in the **Address Bar.**
Clearing Browsing History	You can control the privacy settings by deleting the history of the sites you have browsed. Tapping this option deletes the following information: • The sites that you visited • Passwords that you might have saved. • Personal information that you included in the forms. In case you want to delete browsing data for a specific site only, tap **Individual Website Data,** and then tap on that specific website to delete all the data.
Accept Cookies	This option is enables by default but you can turn them on or off.
Enable Location	To provide you with data that is more specific to your region and location, some website ask for your location. In instances when a website wants to use your location information, Silk Browser will prompt you. tap **Allow** to send your location data, or press **Decline** to ignore.
Advanced	You can disable or enable advanced features for sites • **Closed Captions:** this option will customize closed caption experience for videos on web with compatible formats including font style, color or size of text. • **Load Images:** this option will allow Silk to immediately load the images. • **Show Security Warning:** Silk will alert you with a warning if there is a problem with the security of the site. • **Enable Javascript:** Some sites may not perform properly if you disable this option because it allows the interactive elements on the website to appear. • **Experimental Streaming Viewer:** enabling this option will allow the Silk to prompt you when a website supports the experimental streaming viewing so that you can enjoy flash videos.
Reset Default Settings	This will wipe all the changes in the settings that you made and reset the browser to its default settings.

Chapter 5 – Managing Files on Kindle

Managing files on Your Kindle Fire HDX is very simple. In this section we will be discussing in detail about using E-mail to send files from Kindle Fire HDX, transferring data using USB cable and using Wi-Fi explorer application to transfer files. Read along to get acquainted with these simple yet useful features of Kindle Fire HDX.

Sending Files via E-Mail

Sending Files

To send files using your email on Kindle, you need to attach files to the email first. Take the following steps to attach files on your email:

1. Tap **Attach** option when you are done typing the email.
2. Tap Quickoffice option to attach a personal document, or Gallery to add a video or a picture.
3. Tap on the file, picture, or video that you want to send to add it on your email. And then press **Send.**

Note: 20 MB is the size limit of the files that you send via email.

Transferring Files Using Charging Cable

You can use a USB cable to transfer a lot of content from your Mac or Windows Computer including documents, photos, videos, and music. When attached to your computer via USB cable, your Kindle will appear as **Removable Mass Storage Device.**

Requirements of System:

1. **USB Port:** USB hub attached to an available port or an available USB port.
2. **Macintosh:** Mac OS X 10.6 supported on hardware that is Intel based (and 3.3.x AIR version)
3. **Windows:** Windows 2000 or later.

To download a purchased newspaper, magazine, or book to your Kindle using a USB, go to **Manage Your Kindle** and search for the file you want to download.

The content that you purchase from the Kindle store can be downloaded to devices compatible with Kindle or Kindle Fire HDX as long the device is registered to your Amazon account used to purchase the downloaded content. Follow the given steps to download content using the USB cable:

1. To select "Download & Transfer via USB" press the "Actions" button present beside the title.

Screenshot Courtesy: Amazon.com

2. Select the name of the Kindle compatible device that you want to transfer the file to and press "Download" button.

Screenshot Courtesy: Amazon.com

In case you have not purchased the item that you want to transfer, you can select "Transfer via Computer" when buying the item from Kindle store, and then press "Buy now with 1-Click."

Screenshot Courtesy: Amazon.com

In case you have more than once device registered to your Amazon account, a pop-up window will appear asking you to choose the name of the device. In case you select the wrong name, then you will not be able to open the content on the device.

3. When you have saved the file successfully on your computer than proceed to Transferring content via USB for the rest of the instructions.

Instruction to Transfer the Content

Follow the given instructions to transfer files to your Kindle:

1. Once connected to the computer, your Kindle device will appear in the same place where External USB drives appear usually. For people with Mac the device can be seen on the desktop, while people with Windows can access the device from "My Computer", or "Computer" menu.

2. You might need to unlock your Kindle device before you can access it on your computer. Unlock it and open Kindle drive to access folders.

3. Locate the file that you want to transfer and then drag and drop it to the destination folder such as Pictures, Videos, Music, or Documents.

4. Before unplugging the USB cable make sure that you safely eject the device from your computer.

You can easily find the transferred content in the folder that you transferred it to. Your Kindle device might not recognize the transferred file if:

1. The transferred file is a Supported File Type.

2. Files were not transferred to the correct folder according to their file type.

3. Files do not contain DRM software.

Using Wi-Fi File Explorer Application

Wi-Fi file explorer application allows you to transfer files wirelessly. To transfer files using a USB cable you will have to buy a USB cable separately because it does not come with the Kindle Fire tablet. If you want to avoid buying an extra cable for transferring files you can transfer files wirelessly using Wi-Fi Explorer Pro. Follow the given steps to use Wi-Fi File Explorer to transfer file from your computer to Kindle Fire or vice versa:

1. Tap "Apps" icon on your Kindle Fire.

2. Go to the Kindle Store and search for "Wi-Fi File Explorer Pro" and download it to your Kindle device. Make sure that you download the pro version if you want to enjoy all the features of the application.

3. Once downloaded start the application on your Kindle Fire HDX. At the bottom of the application an http:// will be showing. Go to Internet Explorer in your PC and type the given URL in the address window including the http://.

   The important thing to note is to start Wi-Fi explorer Pro on your tablet before you type the URL in your PC.

   The Wi-Fi explorer program running on your Kindle and the URL working on your PC will allow you to transfer files from your PC to your Kindle tablet.

4. Click the option of "Create Directory" to create a new one. A window will pop-up allowing you to give a name to your directory. Once you have created a directory double click on it to enter the directory. Make sure to be inside the new directory before making any transfers from your PC.

5. To send a file from your PC to your Kindle tap on the highlighted link names 'Select Files.' You can find this window in the right hand corner of the screens of your PC.

6. Search for the files that you want to send to your tablet and click the "Upload File" button. This will allow the file in your PC to be transferred to your Kindle using the Wi-Fi connection in your house.

Follow these simple steps to transfer files from your PC to your Kindle Fire without buying a USB cable.

Chapter 6 - Emails

Setting Up Your Email

To access e-mails on your Kindle you need to tap the option of Applications on the Home screen once your tablet is connected to the internet wirelessly, then tap on the built-in email app on your Kindle Fire to get started.

Setting up E-Mail

Follow the given steps to set up your email account on Kindle Fire:

1. On the setup screen you will see a Start option, tap that to get started with the rest of the setup. The first thing that you need to do is to select the e-mail provider that you currently use.
2. Enter the login information of the email account.
3. You will be required to choose a name which the recipients will see when you send them emails through the email app. You can also name the account in the following way:
   1. If you select **Send mail from this account by default** setting then emails will be sent through this account whenever you use this email application to send messages.
   2. If you select the **Import contacts** option then all the contact from your email account will be available and imported on the email application.

4. To view all the emails in your account, tap **View your inbox** icon.

Viewing E-Mail

When you access the email application, you can view that messages that you have in your e-mail account. To view older emails, scroll to the bottom of the list of emails and tap of view 25 more to see 25 more emails in your account.

1. In the top right corner of the screen, there is a dropdown menu, which contains options to allow you to filter the emails by Subject, Oldest, Newest, and more. You can search for an email by typing your search term in the search field.
2. In order to flag an email, tap on the flag icon.
3. In order to access new messages, tap on the sync icon on the screen.
4. To view additional folders inside your email account such as sent items, outbox, and junk email etc. tap on the menu button.

Creating E-Mail

You can create and email by following the given steps:

1. To create a new email message tap on the **New Message** icon present at the bottom of your tablet's screen.
2. Attach a file by tapping the attach file icons on top of the keyboard you can save your message to drafts, send it, or cancel. To close the keyboard tap on the onscreen keyboard icon.

Downloading Files

Follow the given steps to download attachments when viewing your emails:

1. In order to download attachment, press "Download Complete Message" at the base of your tablet's screen.
2. Tap save in you want to download the attachment to your device, or add Open if you want to view it only.
3. You can find the attached document in Quickoffice, or the downloaded Video, or Picture in Gallery.

Emptying Trash

Access the trash can folder from the Menu at the bottom of the screen. Once you are in the trash can folder tap Menu icon again and select Empty Trash.

Use Microsoft Exchange

Following are the instructions that you can follow to access your calendar, contacts, and emails using your Kindle Fire HD:

1. Unlock your Kindle tablet and make sure that you have a secure Wi-Fi connection.
2. Tap Apps and then Email on the home screen.
3. If you have not setup an email account already then tap Exchange calendar, contacts, and emails. If you have one or more than one accounts on Kindle then tap on the icon of menu, then settings, tap add account, and then exchange calendar, contacts, and email.
4. On the page of Add Exchange Account, type in your name. Type your full email address in the address box, and correct password in the password box and then click "Next".
5. Exchange Server Setting Screen will appear next and you will see that the information is already filled in on your behalf. You might need to change some of the information.
6. In Exchange server window type the name of the Exchange server. In case you are connecting to Office 365, the server name will be outlook.office365.com.
   1. Leave the Domain box empty.
   2. Type your full email address in the Username column.
   3. Type in your complete and correct password in the Password column.
   4. Make sure SSL (secure connection) is selected. Do not select anything except the SSL certificate.
   5. Tap "Next."

7. Remote security admin warning might appear on your window. Read the warning carefully and then press "OK."

Exchange Server Name will automatically control some of the features of security of your tablet.

8. On the page of Synchronization options, tap the calendar and contacts checkbox if you want to synchronize these to your device. Press "Save."

Note: Calendar, contacts, and emails, are synchronized to your device by default. Synchronization of the emails is a must and cannot be turned off.

9. Press "View Inbox" once the setup is complete in order to access your emails. In case you want to change or review the setting of your account tap go to Account Settings.

All about Email Setting

Following are some more Email options that you can make use of in order to make the most of the email options on your Kindle Fire.

Managing Email Accounts

To see all the accounts that you have added in the E-mail application, press on the menu icon present at the base of the screen and then select **Accounts**. By doing this you will also be seeing all the new messages in all the email accounts that have been added to the email application.

Adding an Account

To add another email account in the Email application, press the menu icon and then Add Account. You will have to follow the same steps just like adding the first email account.

Removing an Account

To remove an email account from the email app on Kindle, follow the given simple steps:

1. Access menu at the bottom of the screen and then add **Accounts.**
2. Press the account that you want to remove and hold for two seconds to access additional options.
3. Tap the option of "Remove Account" and then press "OK."

Chapter 7 – Multimedia

In this section you will learn about how to use various Multimedia options in your Kindle fire HDX.

Making and Playing Personal Videos

Recording videos on Kindle Fire HDX is very simple. To access camera, click on Photos on the Home screen of your Kindle Tablet and then tap on the following icon.

Screenshot Courtesy: Amazon.com

You can switch your camera to video making mode by clicking on the following icon.

Screenshot Courtesy: Amazon.com

Once you are in the video recording mode tap on the following icon to start recording videos.

Screenshot Courtesy: Amazon.com

When you start recording a video a counter will show on the screen showing the length of the recorded video. Press the volume buttons if you want to zoom in or out. You can also pinch the screen with your thumb and forefingers in order to zoom. You can stop recording by tapping the same button.

Your Kindle Fire HDX even allows you to take a picture while you are recording a picture. You can do this by tapping the shutter icon that appears on the left side of the screen while you are recording. To focus on a specific location while recording you just need to tap on the screen.

Note: To see the most recent videos and images you can tap on **Camera Roll.** You can swipe right and left through camera roll to move through the captured images and videos.

Streaming and Downloading YouTube Videos

Streaming YouTube videos on Kindle Fire HDX is very simple. So simple that all you have to do is open the silk browser and enter URL www.youtube.com and stream any video that you would like to watch. To enhance the video watching experience you can choose HD modes such as 720p or 1080p. However, you cannot download these videos and therefore you might find it a hassle to stream the videos that you like again and again. But you have nothing to worry about because we have a solution.

Go to your home screen on Kindle and go to App Store. Search for vTube and download to your Kindle Fire. This application has been specifically designed for Kindle Fire for superfast video streaming and downloading videos from YouTube for offline viewing.

Save Memories in Cloud Drive

Screenshot Courtesy: Amazon.com

No matter how much storage space you have on a gadget, it is just not enough. And with so many applications, books, videos, songs, movies, and games that you can download on your Kindle you might feel the need of having more space on your tablet. Moreover if you want to view your content such as images or playlists on multiple devices, it is a hassle to transfer content using a USB flash drive, a USB cable or a hard drive.

With cloud drive you no longer have to worry about transferring your content or deleting it when you don't have enough space. You can now store all your data, images, playlist, videos, books and much more in cloud drive and access it anywhere, everywhere and from any device. Now your music and other content are safe in cloud drive even if you delete it from your tablet.

Moving Content

You can easily move your files using cloud drive website by just following the given steps:

1. Visit Amazon Cloud drive
2. You will see a box next to the files that you wish to move. Check that box.
3. Tap the option of **More Action.**
4. Choose the option to move the files that you have selected.
5. Choose the folder where you want to move your files to.
6. Tap on **Move Item(s).**

Sharing Content

It is very easy to share files on cloud drive. To see the types of files you can share you can read the Cloud Drive's Terms of Use. To share files you need to follow the given steps:

1. Visit the website of cloud drive on your computer or tablet.
2. There will be check boxes next to the files. Check on the file that you want to share.
3. TO copy the URL of the file that you want to share, click the drop down menu of **More Action** and tap on **Share. Shared Files** list will show you the list of files that you are currently sharing.
4. Paste the URL in an email, or any social media to share the content.

View Cloud Drive Content on Your Kindle, Anywhere and Everywhere

What would you do if you need a document on your Kindle while you are travelling, but you have left it at home in your laptop? What about sharing photos with your loved ones during vacations but they are not on your tablet? You want to listen to a song but you don't have that on your tablet because you downloaded it on your PC. Well now we have a perfect way of avoiding such situations. Upload the content on your cloud drive and you can access it from anywhere and everywhere.

Screenshot Courtesy: Amazon.com

Viewing photos that you have uploaded on Cloud Drive is very easy; just follow the given steps to access your photos from anywhere:

1. Open your Cloud account to access the photos that you have uploaded in cloud drive. The account that you used to register on Cloud Drive should be the same as that you used for registering on Kindle Fire HDX in order to see the photos.
2. Click **Device** to access the photos that you have downloaded Kindle or captured using the front facing camera.
3. Navigate the Images library to access the images.
4. Tap on the albums to open them.
5. To zoom images, using your forefinger and thumb to pinch inwards or outwards to zoom in or out respectively.
6. Hold the tablet in portrait mode to view the images in grid view.
7. To see the images in mosaic view, hold the tablet in landscape mode.

Chapter 8 – Kindle Applications

You can download any application you want on your Kindle Fire from Amazon Appstore. You can search for the applications that you are looking for and download them instantly. There is also an option of **Free App of the Day** that you can use to download one paid application per day. In this section we will be discussing more about adding and deleting applications on Kindle fire HDX.

Adding Applications

In order to buy paid applications from Amazon Appstore you need to set up an account first. To search for applications that you want to download tap **Apps** on the home screen of your Kindle Fire and then go to **Store.**

On the home page of Amazon you will find Free app of the day, featured apps, and best sellers etc. you can also search for the application that you are looking for in the search bar.

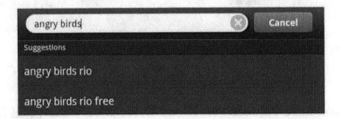

Screenshot Courtesy: Amazon.com

You can also find an app through the following methods:

1. Browsing the appstore by categories that you interested in such as games, lifestyle, newspaper and magazines, business, book, and a lot more.
2. You can find application through the recommendations. To view the recommendations you need to log in to your Amazon account.

Once you have found the application that you want to purchase. Simply tap the price button in orange and press **Get app** or **Buy app.** When you tap this option, the amount of the application will be automatically deducted from your 1-click payment method. No amount will be charged if the application that you want to download is free. Press **Open** to start the application.

Screenshot Courtesy: Amazon.com

In case you like an application but want to purchase it at some later time, then press **Save** in order to add the application to "Saved for Later" list. You can access this list by tapping the **Menu** icon, then tapping **More,** and then choosing **Saved for Later** option.

Download and installation of an application starts automatically once you purchase the application on Kindle. To download application that you had previously purchased click on the **Cloud** tab.

1. Click **Apps** on the home screen of your Kindle Fire.
2. Tap and hold the application that you want to download on your tablet and then click **Install.**

Screenshot Courtesy: Amazon.com

Managing Applications

You can view and update applications in the **Apps** library.

1. To **Update your Applications** tap **Store** from **Apps**. Then tap the **Menu** icon. Click on **App Updates**. You can update each application separately by tapping update or you can select the option of **Update All.**

2. To view all the applications that you have downloaded on your Kindle Fire. Tap **Apps** on home screen and click on the option of device. This will show you a list of all the applications that you have uploaded on your device. The **Cloud** tab will show you all the applications that you have purchased previously and can download again on your tablet.

Removing Applications

It is very easy to remove applications from your Kindle Fire HDX if you are not using them anymore. All you have to do is follow the given steps:

1. Tap **Apps** on home screen.
2. Tap **Device** to see the list of all the applications that are downloaded on your device.
3. Tap and hold the application that you want to remove and then click on **Remove from Device.**

Downloaded apps that you delete from your device will still be available on the **Cloud** tab in case you want to download the deleted applications again.

To delete the application permanently visit **Your Apps** on your web browser. Click the dropdown menu of **Actions** on the right of the application and then click on "Delete this app." Permanently deleting an app will require you to purchase it again in order to download it on your device in the future.

Troubleshooting

Troubleshooting involves either determining a problem or solving it. When faced with a problem on your Kindle Fire you can log onto Amazon.com and visit Kindle Support center. Following are the answers of some of the most commonly faced problems on Kindle:

Downloading Application

Problem

The downloading didn't start even after you purchased the application.

Solution

1. Check the internet connection of your tablet.

   The download or installation of an application may have dropped due to poor internet connection.

2. Once you get a strong Wi-Fi connection, press "Apps" on the home screen of your tablet, select "Cloud" from the application library. Hold and press the application that you want to download and tap "Install."

Problem

You can get an error stating that your device does not have enough memory when you try to download an application.

Solution

This error means that you do not have enough memory on your device to add any new file. In order to fix this error you need to delete some of the content from your device. In order to delete previously installed files, tap and press the icon of the application and tap "delete." You can download this application in the future from Cloud drive. Once you have vacated enough memory try downloading the application again.

Problem

You are unable to download the application from Cloud.

Solution

Date & Time

1. Tap **Quick Setting** on home screen and then click **More.** Click **Date & Time** and then turn on the automatic settings.
2. Check your Wi-Fi for compatibility.
3. Kindle Fire is not compatible with peer-to-peer or ad-hoc wireless networks.
    1. Hidden networks
    2. Your Kindle will connect to WPA EAP, WPA2 PSK, PSK, WEP, and WPA2 EAP encrypted networks.
    3. N, G, and B routers

Check internet connectivity

1. Check internet connection on any device other than your Kindle.
2. Turning off the modem and router solves most of the Wi-Fi connection problems.
3. Unplug the power of both the modem and the router and wait for 30 seconds.
4. Power up the modem again and wait until it boots.
5. Power up the router and wait for it to boot too.

Restart Kindle

Minor issues in Kindle can be easily resolved by turning it off and back on.

1. Press the **Power** button for 20 seconds.
2. Release the button after 20 seconds.
3. Press the power button again in order to restart Kindle.

Applications

Problem

Application is not working up to your expectations.

Solution

Contact customer service to resolve issues with applications.

Problem

How to add reviews for applications?

Solution

Visit the application's page and click **Reviews** and then select **Create Your Own Review.**

Chapter 9 – Camera

Using Camera on Kindle Fire HDX is extremely easy. However, you should know that the videos you record and the pictures you take are automatically stored in Cloud Drive and accounts for storage space. If you want to change this setting then swipe the screen from left edge and click on **Settings**, and then turn off the Automatic Upload option.

In this section we will discuss in detail the use of camera on Kindle Fire HDX and the ways to enhance its result and transferring the images to other devices.

Using Camera

1. To access camera, click **Photos** on the **Home Screen** and then tap the icon of the camera.

Screenshot Courtesy: Amazon.com

2. To switch to video mode, or camera mode click the following icon.

Screenshot Courtesy: Amazon.com

3. To turn the flash Off, On, or on Auto click the following icon.

Screenshot Courtesy: Amazon.com

4. Use the following icon to switch between front and rare facing camera.

Note: to capture images that are wide ranged and panoramic you need to use to rare facing camera. To capture panoramic images click **Setting > Panorama** and then take the picture by slowly moving the camera horizontally or vertically to take a panoramic image.

5. Click the following icon to switch the setting between HDR (High Dynamic Range) and Panoramic.

Tip: HDR settings capture three images at the same time; one at a short range to capture the bright aspect of the scene, second at a longer range to capture people's faces, and the third is a normal image. All these images are combined to properly depict the darker and brighter aspects of the scene. In HDR only the final image is saved and not the original ones, so in case you want to save the original images too turn on "Keep Original Image" option on in the system camera settings. Open the drop down menu on home screen and tap on **quick settings,** then click **settings > applications > camera.**

6. In order to access **Film Strip** turn your tablet to landscape orientation and then tap **Camera Roll.** Tap and hold any video or photo in the **Strip** to share a stack of images, multiple images, or video all at the same time.

    To see a preview of the video or an image tap it in **Film Strip** and then tap and hold if you want to delete, share, or edit it.

    In order to close **Film Strip** tap the icon of **Camera Roll** and tilt the tablet in portrait mode.

7. You can take a picture by tapping the following icon.

Screenshot Courtesy: Amazon.com

Tap in order to focus a certain location in the image preview in the front camera.

Tap in the screen in order to focus on a certain location.

Press the volume buttons on the tablet to zoom in and out or use two fingers to pinch the screen in and out.

Tip: in order to take a stack of pictures tap and hold this icon. Counter of the number of images taken by the device will be shown next to this icon.

8. Tap the menu button in order to view additional options such as **Print** or information about the image or the video.

Screenshot Courtesy: Amazon.com

9. Tap the following icon to share the captured image or video.

Screenshot Courtesy: Amazon.com

In case you want to delete videos or photos in order to free some storage space on your device you can do so by accessing the photos library. To delete an image or a video you need to take the following steps:

1. To delete a video or a photo from Cloud Drive or from Kindle Fire HDX, tap and hold the thumbnail of the image and tap **Delete.**

2. You can also delete multiple photos and videos at the same time by tapping Select icon and then selecting all the images and the videos that you want to delete. After you are done selecting tap delete icon.

Note: you can also use the cameras on Kindle Fire HDX to make video calls in applications like Skype. You can download Skype from Amazon App store in order to stay connected to your loved ones.

Enhance the Result of Kindle Camera with Additional Applications

There are many applications available on Amazon app store that you can download on your Kindle Fire HDX to enhance the result of the camera or to edit the images that you take through your camera. We will be discussing two such applications in this part of the book.

myCamera HD: Kindle Fire Camera

Screenshot Courtesy: Amazon.com

This application allows you to take pictures and record videos on your Kindle Fire HDX. You can use this application to capture images in different scene modes such as party, sunset, night, action, or auto. It also allows you to adjust the white balance of your pictures. To Quick Shoot you can open this application in Camera mode, and can press the top button in your tablet for Handy Shoot.

Photo Editor

Screenshot Courtesy: Amazon.com

You can use this image to edit photos that you took using your Kindle Fire HDX. This application allows you to:

1. Add clone, frames, resize, crop, rotate, add colors and effects, and you can even draw on the images.

2. It allows you to fine tune the colors of the images.

3. In drawing mode you can add images or text in your picture.

4. You can rotate, resize, or crop the pictures.

5. It allows you to save images in different formats such as PNG or JPEG.

6. You can save the edited images in your Kindle photo gallery and you can also share them on any social networks such as Facebook, or Twitter.

Transferring Pictures and Videos from Your Kindle to Computer

You can transfer images from your Kindle Fire HDX to your PC through a USB cable or Wi-Fi explorer application in the same way as discussed in the previous section of the book. You can even share images on Twitter or Facebook in the following way:

1. Click on Photos, on the Home screen of your Kindle device.
2. To access the categories under, **Photos** or **Sources**, swipe the left edge of the screen.
3. Tap on the video or the image that you want to share.
4. Tap the following icon to share.

Screenshot Courtesy: Amazon.com

Tap **E-mail** to email your videos or images.

Tap the Facebook icon in order to share the image or video on Facebook. You can even tag the people on the image before sharing.

Tap Twitter icon to share images on Twitter, you will have to add a 140 character or less tweet in order to share.

Note: you can also share multiple images or video at a time by selecting all the images that you want to share then click on the same icon and then choose Email, Facebook, or More option.

Chapter 10 – Print from Kindle

To Print from Kindle Fire HDX you need a printer that supports printing from mobile devices. If it does then you can print PDF, PowerPoint, Excel or Word documents from your tablet.

Note: documents that have been converted to (.azw) kindle format cannot be printed.

To print using your Kindle Fire HDX you first need to install a plug-in on your tablet from Amazon application store. You can find a plug-in for various printer brands on app store.

After you are done downloading and installing the plug-in you need to make sure that the printed is switched on and connected to Wi-Fi in order to start printing.

1. Tap and hold the document that you want to print and then select **Print.**
2. This will show you the list of printers, select your printer from the list and click **Connect.** Press refresh button if you cannot find your printer in the list. You can also add your printer manually by clicking the plus on top of the screen.

Screenshot Courtesy: Amazon.com

3. Tap on **More Options** to choose Orientation, Paper size, or Color Mode. You can also select a number for the number of copies that you want to print.

Screenshot Courtesy: Amazon.com

4. Select **Print** to start printing.

Chapter 11 – Power and Battery

In this section we will discuss how you can charge and conserve battery power on Kindle Fire HDX.

Charging Battery

You can change your tablet with the micro-USB cable and adapter that came with the device. With the adapter the tablet will be fully charged in just less than 6 hours.

Important: it is preferable that you choose the adapter that came with the device. Using a different power adapter or USB cable, or charging the device through your computer will increase the time needed to completely charge Kindle Fire HDX.

To charge the tablet simply connect the cable to your device and to the adapter and then plug the adapter in a power outlet.

Note: the cable might appear slanted when you are charging the device but that is to facilitate you to hold the tablet while the device is charging.

To indicate that the tablet is charging a lightning bolt will appear in the battery indicator. If you cannot see this sign it means that the tablet is not charging.

Screenshot Courtesy: Amazon.com

Conserving Battery

You can prolong your battery life by changing some of the settings and turning off some of the features of your tablet. The battery works up to 12 to 18 hours depending on the use of the tablet. Following are some of the tips that you can use in order to increase the battery life.

1. **Use Headphones** – to avoid the extended use of speaker of your Kindle, connect your headphones to the headphone jack.

2. You can adjust the time out of the screen - tap the drop down menu on the top of the screen and select **Quick Settings > Settings > Display & Sounds > Display Sleep** and decrease the times that it takes you Kindle to go in Sleep Mode when it is not being used.

3. In case you do not need wireless then turn it off by tapping the drop down menu on top of the screen. Open **Quick settings > Wireless** then tap on next to the **Airplane Mode.**

4. Tap on the drop down menu on the top of the screen and then tap **Quick Setting > Brightness.** Swipe right and left to decrease or increase the brightness.

5. To stop notifications select go to the drop down menu on top of the screen and click on **Quick setting > Settings > Notification and Quiet Time.** Choose the application that you want to stop the notification from and then tap **Quiet Time.**

Total Percentage of Battery

The battery indicator on top of the tablet's screen indicates the total battery life left. To can see the exact percentage of the battery left for accurate battery details. To see the percentage you need to:

1. Tap on the drop down menu of top of the screen and open **Quick Settings** and then click on **Settings.**
2. Select **Device.**
3. Tap On next to the **Show Battery Percentage in the Status Bar** option.

Screenshot Courtesy: Amazon.com

You will able to see the percentage of the battery left next to the battery indicator.

Chapter 12 – Security

You can change the security setting of your device to stop any unauthorized access to your personal data.

Create a PIN or Lock Screen Password

When you switch on your Kindle Fire HDX or wake it after sleep mode a lock screen appears. The lock screen display the notifications and current date and time. If your device is not password or PIN protected then anyone can enter your tablet and access your personal data. Follow the given steps to protect your tablet:

1. Tap on the drop down menu on top of the screen and tap on **Quick Settings,** and then select **Settings.**
2. Click on **Security**.
3. Select On, next to the **Lock Screen Password.** You can add a numeric password or you can set a difficult password with a combination of special characters, letters, and numbers. Such a combination creates a stronger password than just letter or numbers.

Parental Controls

To restrict the access of children to some features of Kindle Fire HDX you can use the option of parental control. In the Parental control screen you can either create a password for parental control or create a profile in Kindle Free Time. This allows you to create a separate profile for your children with a daily time limit to give them access to only kid-friendly content. Follow the given steps in order to do so:

1. Access **Quick Settings** by tapping on the top of the screen and then go to **Settings.**
2. Click **Parental Controls.**
3. Click **Open Kindle Free Time.** This will give you access to Kindle Free Time app or simple turn **On** the **Parental Controls.**
4. After you turn on **Parental Controls** you can enter a password and confirm it by resubmitting it, and then tap **Submit.** You can restrict one or all of the following options buy setting the password.

   Services that are Location Based

   Wireless connectivity

   Special types of content such as applications or books

   Access to movies and TV shows on Amazon Instant Video

   Ability to purchase content

   Camera

   Sharing on social networks

   Calendar apps, contacts, and emails

   Browsing on net

A lock sign will appear on the top of the screen after you turn on the **Parental Controls.**

Screenshot Courtesy: Amazon.com

Chapter 13- Kindle Fire HDX Tricks and Traps

Following are two amazing tricks and traps that you can do on your Kindle fire HDX to enhance your overall tablet experience.

When using the touch keyboard we can never be sure whether we touched a particular letter or not while typing and this may lead us to make unnecessary typing mistakes. Well now we have a solution for that. You can turn on the sound of the keyboard so that whenever you hit a key a sound will be made telling you whether or not you have entered the letter you tapped on not. This is how you can do it.

1. Tap on the top of the screen to access the drop down menu and then tap **Keyboards.**
2. Go to **Keyboard Settings.**
3. Turn **On** the **Sound On Key Press**

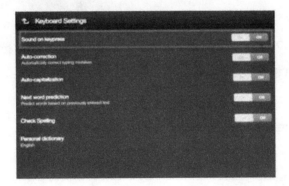

It can be really annoying when you are reading a book on your Kindle Fire HDX and suddenly the brightness in dimmed in 30 to 60 seconds because you are not touching the screen every minute. While it is good for the battery life if your tablet goes to sleep in 30 second to a minute but this can be annoying when you are reading a book. To change the settings and eliminate this problem you need to follow the given steps.

1. Tap on the top of the screen to access the drop down menu.
2. Tap **Settings.**
3. Go to **Display & Sounds.**
4. Click **Display Sleep** and then select the time that you want.

Using Mayday on Kindle

Screenshot Courtesy: Amazon.com

Mayday is an amazing feature on Kindle Fire HDX that sets it apart from all the other tablets out there. It is a customer care feature that will help you fix any problem that you might face. To access Mayday all you have to do tap on the drop down menu on top of the screen and tap on the Mayday icon at the top right corner of the screen. A few seconds after tapping the icon an Amazon advisor will pop-up in a window on your screen. You can see and talk to the advisor while they can talk to you but not see you. They will ask your permission before accessing your tablet. You can tell them about any trouble that you are facing with your tablet and they will tell you how to fix it in no time.

Get Rid Of Advertisements

If you bought the "With Special Offer" version of the tablet then you are stuck with a version with advertisements and they will soon annoy you. To get rid of the advertisements you will have to part with $15. Follow the simple steps and you will not be disturbed with anymore advertisements.

1. Log in to your account on Amazon.
2. Click on Manage Your Devices.
3. Click on Edit under Special Offers.
4. Tap next to Subscribed and press next again to go to Device and then click Unsubscribe.

In case you want to turn off the recommendations also you can do so by clicking on Settings > Applications > Amazon Home > Recommendations and then click Hide.

Install Application Apart From Amazon Appstore

You might find the collection of applications on Amazon Appstore slightly limited as compared to Google play. There are more than 700,000 applications on Google play for android while only some of these are available on Amazon. There is a very simple way of downloading applications from Google play without having to root your device which will void the warranty. Before enabling Installation of Apps from Other Sources in your device settings you should download and install a security app for Android.

Tap on the drop down menu and click on Settings and then go to Applications. Turn On Installing Applications from other sources. This will allow you to download APK files on your tablet. You can directly download them on your device or email them to your device. Click on the list of alternate android app store to get the list of sites from where you can download applications on your tablet apart from the Amazon app store.

If you have another device such as an android smart phone on which you can access Google play then you can download games and application you want on that device and then copy them to your PC with the help of a File Explorer application. Copy these file on your Kindle Fire HDX tablet and then use File Explorer to search them and install them on your tablet. To share files wirelessly you can also make use of Dropbox.

Watch Kindle Content on HDTV

One of the best features of Kindle Fire HDX is that you can connect it to your HDTC and watch movies, videos, photos, or TV series on the big screen. Buy a HDMI or Micro HDMI cable and plug in your TV. There are two ways of sharing content wirelessly also:

Second Screen

This is a feature in Kindle Fire HDX which will allow you to share content wirelessly. After sharing screen via Wi-Fi the tablet will serve as a remote control or a second screen with more information. You can play Kindle content on Play Station 4, Play Station 3 and 2013 and beyond models of Samsung TV. In order to start sharing content you first need to sign in to Instant Video Application from the tablet using your account email and password.

Now with you start a TV series or a Movie you will see a Second Screen option on the screen of your tablet. Tap this icon to share content on a big screen. The Instant Video App should also be running on the big screen in order to start sharing.

Once the content is shared you can use your tablet as remote control or to see more information such as X-Ray option or you can continue with other tasks on the tablet such as browsing internet without disrupting the shared content.

Miracast

Miracast is a certified mirroring device that you can use to share content on the big screen. Wi-Fi network is not required to share content using Miracast. If you have this device then sharing is fairly simple; just click on Settings > Display and Sounds > Display mirroring and your Kindle tablet will scan the areas for a compatible device. Tap connect when it locates the device and now you should be able to watch your content on another screen. While the screen is being mirrored you will not be able to use your Kindle Fire HDX for any other purpose as it will disrupt the mirroring.

Watch Flash Videos

The Silk Browser on Kindle Fire HDX does not support Flash Videos so in order to play Flash videos you need to make some changes.

1. Click on Settings and then go to Applications.
2. Turn on the option of Apps from Other Sources.
3. The third thing you need is a File Explorer Application.
4. Search for Flash Player APK files and Dolphin HD on internet.
5. Load APK files on your tablet and then with the help of the File Explorer tap to install first the Dolphin HD and then the Flash Player.

Get More Storage

Kindle Fire HDX has 16 GB or 32 GB storage which might not be enough depending upon the use of the tablet. However, the storage can be increased by Cloud or hardware devices. With Amazon Cloud Drive comes 5 GB of free storage device. Other cloud services such as Box, SugarSync, and Dropbox can also be used to expand the storage memory. Furthermore you can also buy an external Hard Drive.

Conclusion

Kindle Fire HDX is an amazing tablet to work with. It comes loaded with features that have placed it among the top grossing tablets in the market. It allows you to watch movies, read books, play high definition games, take photos, record videos, share photos and videos, email, browse the internet, download and stream videos, and set parental controls. You name it and Kindle Fire HDX has it.

This is the reason why we compiled for you the tips, tricks and traps guide about Kindle Fire HDX so that you can maximize your experience while using the tablet. We have tried to answer any question and trouble that you might have had in this book so that you can sit back and enjoy the amazing features of Kindle Fire HDX.

So, if you don't have Kindle Fire HDX already then go on Amazon and buy it right now and if you have it then read this guide to enter the amazing world of HDX and to get mesmerized by its extraordinary features.

www.ingramcontent.com/pod-product-compliance
Lightning Source LLC
Chambersburg PA
CBHW060451060326
40689CB00020B/4493